DEATH OF A SAVIOUR

Michael Collins

Death of a Saviour

REFLECTIONS ON GOOD FRIDAY

the columba press

First published in 2013 by
the columba press
55A Spruce Avenue, Stillorgan Industrial Park,
Blackrock, Co. Dublin

Cover by Bill Bolger
Origination by The Columba Press
Printed by MPG Books Group Limited

ISBN 978 1 78218 022 7

Contents

Stations of the Cross

The First Station
The Second Station
The Third Station
The Four Station
The Five Station
The Six Station
The Seven Station
The Eight Station
The Nine Station
The Ten Station
The Eleven Station
The Twelfth Station

Introduction

Dear Reader,

Back in my childhood the whole world ground to a halt on Good Friday. Well, perhaps not the whole world, but the world that I knew. All work was halted, shops were closed, no newspapers were published, radio stations closed down, or if not, they stuck to a diet of grey and sombre music all day long. Catholics went to church for the Stations of the Cross at three o'clock and perhaps later for what were called the Easter Ceremonies. As an act of repentance for their sins they ate little food and no meat and in general took a consciously reverent approach to the whole day.

With that kind of background, you can understand why I might make a few false assumptions about your familiarity with the events of this day. I live in hope that my assumptions are correct, perhaps because I tend to fool myself that we are still a Christian nation. However, let me just summarise the essentials of the Christian faith.

Nearly 2000 years ago a man called Jesus Christ was executed by crucifixion in the City of Jerusalem on this day which we call Good Friday. He was a very holy man and a great spiritual teacher but that counted for little. There were many other holy men in His time and since. What set Him apart was that He claimed to be the Son of God – not in any figurative or adoptive sense, but that He was generated directly by God and so was the image and the equal of God. He preached love for one another, non-violence, forgiveness, love of your enemies, respect for women, compassion for sinners, care for the sick and lonely, and respect for lawful authority; and He issued a warning to the rich and powerful that their time was running out. Naturally enough the rich and powerful took a very dim view of this and condemned Him to death as a troublemaker, and, as I said, executed Him by crucifixion on Good Friday.

We Christians happen to think that He was the Son of God and that He was right about what He preached, and that He founded a church to continue His work down the ages. We cannot compel you to believe any of this. We can only present you with the evidence and that evidence is fairly compelling. After all, there is stronger evidence that Jesus proved His claim to be the Son of God than there is that Julius Caesar conquered Gaul, but the human race was never known for its reliance on logic or reason.

God sent His son into the world to make our lives here on earth better, to turn us away from behaviour that messes up other people's lives and to bring us to an eternally peaceful life after death. We didn't listen to Him then, and we let Him die. It's time for us to start listening again.

Michael Collins
Feeny, Lent 2013

Good Friday I

The Politicians

In my youth and innocence I used to believe that men were put to death for their religious beliefs. That was how we came to have 'martyrs for the faith', whatever their particular brand of faith might be.

More recently I have come to realise that it was not their religious beliefs but their political statements that brought men to the stake, to the gallows or the guillotine. They may indeed have started out with the firm intention of avoiding anything even remotely political, but if their audience chooses to put a political label on what they are saying then nothing else matters. It is, after all, what you hear and not what I say that counts.

I think it was the story of an American priest, Walter Cizek, that first made me aware of this distinction. He was working in his native Poland when the Second World War broke out, and when the Russians invaded Poland he was arrested as a 'spy for the Vatican', and thrown into the Lubyanka Prison in Moscow.

The charge was so ludicrous, to his mind, that he did not worry unduly about it. He assumed that it was only a matter of time before some more senior officer realised that he was merely a priest and set him free.

Five years of solitary confinement in the Lubyanka, and fifteen years of hard labour in Siberia convinced him that they did not quite see eye to eye with him on this point. They were boringly single-minded and serious about the charge. He was preaching Christianity; Christianity condemned Russian Communism; therefore, he was an enemy of Communism and of the Russian people.

This conflict or, if you like, coincidence of religious beliefs and political doctrines is an eternal problem, and for many it has proved quite fatal. Politics has been aptly described as the 'art of the possible', which means that it is much more concerned with today's possibilities than with yesterday's principles or tomorrow's promises. Indeed, there is so little emphasis on principle that it is tacitly agreed that a politician may not merely betray principles and forget promises but he may break the law itself if he has what he thinks is a good enough reason, as long as he does not get caught.

That kind of thinking was as common in the time of Christ as it is today. It was Christ's misfortune to get involved in the affairs of two politically aware and, we may guess, politically nervous gentlemen – Annas and Pontius Pilate.

They were both ambitious men who had made it a good way up the political ladder, but they were on the same ladder – Pilate slightly higher up than Annas – and if someone started shaking it they were both going to fall down. It was clear, then, that they had to hang on together, or be hanged separately, even though, on a personal level, they could not stand one another. Somehow, they had to protect the fragile system that supported them; and to achieve this they were quite willing to break the laws of the very system they were supposed to be defending.

They had their excuses and, no doubt, they would have defended them vigorously, but since the size of a man's feet or the state of his digestion may offer a better explanation of his actions than vague political forces perhaps we should take a closer look at these two men who made their way into the history books over the dead body of Jesus Christ.

Annas had no official standing among the Jews (at least at the time that concerns us) but everyone knew that he was the power behind the throne. His son-in-law Caiaphas was High Priest, but he was only one in a long line of candidates whom Annas manoeuvred into that high position – among them his five sons and his grandson. He was a greedy man with a sizeable stake in the temple trade in areas such as currency exchange and the sale of animals for sacrifice, and he conducted his business so efficiently that the historian Josephus records that 'there was no one as astute as Annas in enriching himself'.

He was also a politician; therefore, while keeping his own footing at the centre of the political see-saw he had to maintain a balance between all the different groups and parties that made up the swirling mass of his country-men at each end. There were the Pharisees, who we could call the established churchmen of their day; there were the Sadducees, the ruling conservative party; the Essenes, a kind of spiritual-ecology party who had dropped out of the rat-race and retired to the desert; the Zealots, who favoured violent methods to overthrow the power of Rome; and merged and mixed in among them all there was that amorphous mass of ordinary citizens – 'the people of the land', as they were called – ready to be stirred or shaken into action by the latest demagogue with a good line in political slogans.

In charge of all these people – Annas included – was Pontius Pilate, a homesick colonial administrator with an inferiority com-plex and a bad temper. He despised the Jews and their convoluted religious laws and tradi-tions, and wanted nothing more than to punch in his time and get back home to Rome. Officially he was the representative of Roman power in Judea – a kind of Secretary of State following the imposition of direct rule. However, he was at the mercy of every crackpot and conniver who wanted to report him to Rome – not least King Herod, who had a bad name for carrying stories about neighbouring rulers back to the Emperor.

It was into the hands of these two makeshift politicians that the fate of Christ passed. As long as he had confined himself to healing the sick and calling on all men to love God and love their neighbour it was all right. That was religion. Even when he denounced the scribes and Pharisees for laying heavy burdens on men's shoulders and not lifting a finger to help them, they were willing to let it pass. But when he started calling the Jewish leaders hypocrites and whited sepulchres, and accusing them of killing the prophets, and warning them that he would destroy the temple and in three days rebuild it, that was politics; and when it was backed by a crowd of noisy supporters in the capital city – as on Palm Sunday – that was dangerous politics, and something would have to be done about it.

Annas and Pilate were the responsible political authority, and on the face of it they were the guardians of the law, but if it should prove necessary to kill one man in order to keep their system of government intact they had no intention of allowing the law – Jewish or Roman – to get in the way. The result was that in their efforts to clear up the problem of Jesus they coldly and deliberately broke the law whenever it suited them.

Annas and his son-in-law Caiaphas broke the law when they used an informer to arrest Jesus. The Mosaic Law took a dim view of people who, as the Book of Leviticus said, 'whispered calumnies in the public ear and swore away their neighbour's life'. He broke the law by interrogating Jesus privately during the night, for the Talmud – whose teaching stretches right back to the time of Moses – says that all proceedings in which the life of a man is at stake must take place in the full light of day. And this infringement probably gave rise to the next offence because it was when Christ said that there was 'nothing secret' about his teaching – in contrast, we may assume, to the night-time activities of Annas – that the guard hit him across the face, and the Talmud is quite specific about the illegality of striking, or allowing others to strike, a prisoner.

The conduct of the blasphemy charge was illegal, and the announcement that Jesus stood condemned by his own words was illegal, for the law insisted that any admission had to be confirmed by witnesses. The charges before Pilate were illegal because the accusation was changed from blasphemy to inciting the people and condemning taxation right in the middle of the trial, and the final action of Pilate himself was illegal for he broke every law of God and man by condemning an innocent man to death.

We should be consoled by all this evidence that Annas and Pilate – rather than you and I – were responsible for the death of Jesus, but instead of consolation it generates a vague feeling of uneasiness, a shadowy anxiety that we have seen it all before, and that somehow we have had a hand in it.

Political unrest, direct rule, Secretaries of State, security problems, midnight arrests, allegations of torture, intimidation of prisoners, special courts, discredited witnesses, informers – is it not all just a bit too familiar? We cannot help wondering would Christ not have suffered the same fate if he were to come back again to our own country in our own time. But then, maybe he has suffered the same fate again. After all, he did say rather emphatically, 'If you do it to one of the least of these brethren of mine, you do it to me.'

Good Friday II

Four Frightened Men

For a short while on this, the saddest day of the Christian year, we step aside from the busy affairs of life and recall the death of Jesus Christ, the Messiah, the Chosen One.

To the unbeliever, He is merely another religious leader, another man of extremes, telling his followers to sell all they have and give the proceeds to the poor, or inviting persecution by calling the duly appointed leaders of the people 'hypocrites' and 'whited sepulchres'.

To believers, He is the Son of God, descended upon this earth for a short while and taking upon Himself responsibility for the sins and failings of the entire human race. He offers victory over death, and eternal life to them, but they see Him as a threat and they close ranks against him. Annas, Caiaphas, Pilate and Herod all unite to put Him to death on a cross, but they are merely the representatives of the human race. Their sins are our sins, their failings are our failings, and their judgment on the Son of God is merely the same selfish judgment that we all make on Him when we reject His offer of salvation and live our lives according to our own selfish standards.

Annas

The cohort and its captain and the Jewish guards seized Jesus and bound Him. They took Him first to Annas, because Annas was the father-in-law of Caiaphas, who was High Priest that year.

History has not dealt kindly with Annas. Even among his own people his standing was never high. He owed his own appointment to the High Priesthood twenty-seven years previously, to the Roman procurator Quirinius, and even though he had been dismissed from office nine years later he still retained enough influence to have his five sons, one after the other, appointed to the High Priesthood, until the present day when his son-in-law Caiaphas filled the position.

Annas was the power behind the throne, and he made no bones about it. He expected the temple guards and their Roman escort to turn aside with their prisoner when they reached his house, even though he was a private citizen now with no right even to question Jesus, much less to judge Him. But the person of Jesus was not the focus of his attention. It was the disciples of Jesus and the message they would preach that really worried him. If Jesus was merely another religious enthusiast – and they had known plenty of them down the years – then there was nothing to worry about. So the first question Annas put to Jesus was not

'Who are you?' but 'Who are your followers?', and the second was 'What is your message? What are your followers going to tell the world?' He assumed that there was more to the teachings of Jesus than love of God and forgiveness of one's enemies. What was the hidden agenda? In His answer Jesus merely referred him back to the public account of His teaching: 'I have spoken openly for all the world to hear. … I have said nothing in secret. But why ask me? Ask my hearers what I taught: they know what I said.'

This was not what Annas had expected. Prisoners were usually fawning and respectful and anxious to please. But not this Jesus of Nazareth. He defied Annas as though He were a power in the land Himself, with no reason to fear anyone.

The anger which His answer stirred up was clearly visible in the face of Annas, and one of the soldiers struck Jesus across the face. 'Is that how you address the High Priest?'

The reply of Jesus was so measured and subdued that the blow might never have been struck. Others might react to violence with fear or anger, but He was His ever-reasonable self: 'If there is something wrong in what I said, point it out; but if there is no offence in it, why do you strike me?'

With those words the encounter was over and Annas had lost. He had been shown up as a bully and as a schemer. Then, he could only send Jesus on to Caiaphas and hope that the long and wiry arm of the law will finally suppress this plotter and instil fear into the hearts of his followers.

***

The dreams of power have enticed too many of us from the path of truth and sincerity. How many words have we spoken, how many deeds have we done that had power as their final purpose and not the benevolent concern for others that we have displayed to the world. Too often we have been prepared to join in the exploitation of others and the crucifixion of Christ for the sake of another year or even another day in power.

Help us, Lord, to look into our hearts and to see there the selfish drives and desires that shape so much of our effort, and if we can never achieve complete purity of heart, may we at least be honest with ourselves.

Caiaphas

> Then Annas sent Him still bound to Caiaphas
> the High Priest.

Caiaphas was a front man, an actor playing a part written by his father-in-law Annas. His job was to give a coating of respectability and legality to the scheming of Annas. In law, he held the most responsible political and religious post in the community, the equivalent of Prime Minister and Archbishop of Canterbury rolled into one. He was president of the Sanhedrin, the ruling council of the people, with responsibility for every aspect of their spiritual and social lives. He was also the buffer zone between the Jews and their Roman conquerors for he had been appointed to his office by the Roman Procurator, so we must assume that he had some credibility at least with them. In short, the people looked to him to guide them in the service of God, to protect them from their enemies and to promote their growth and well-being as members of the Jewish community.

Caiaphas neglected all these duties. He used the Romans and the law to protect himself and to persecute Jesus.

According to the law a quorum of twenty-three members of the Sanhedrin was necessary to conduct a criminal trial, but since they were judges and not prosecutors someone else had to bring the charges, and the accusations had to be backed by the evidence of at least two witnesses whose testimony must agree in all essentials. It was in the presentation of this evidence and in his handling of the witnesses that Caiaphas showed his incompetence and his dependence on his father-in-law.

He was the quintessential 'spoiled boy', who did what he had to do to protect his own interests and the interests of his family. If it seemed to him that the only way to deal with Christ was to kill Him, then he bluntly told the rest of the ruling classes that they had better face the fact that either one man died or the entire nation was put in jeopardy. The delicate balance of power between the Romans and themselves would inevitably be upset if some fanatic were to lead another futile bid for independence, and not merely would the rebellious nation be crushed without mercy, the high-priestly families would disappear too and with them the influence and the lifestyle of a man like Caiaphas. Jesus had to die or they were all in danger.

Annas, however, was a much more astute individual, and he realised that were Jesus to die a martyr's death there would be uproar among the ordinary people – exactly what he was trying to avoid – and so he passed Jesus over to Caiaphas in the firm hope that he would use the law – Roman or Jewish – to frame Jesus as a criminal and then to have Him sentenced to death.

Caiaphas completely botched the attempt to rig the trial. His witnesses contradicted one another and he had to fall back on the evidence of two who claimed that Jesus had talked of destroying the temple and rebuilding it in three days. Even Caiaphas was not impressed by them, and in exasperation he cut through the legalities and demanded of Jesus, 'I put you on oath by the living God to tell us if you are the Christ, the Son of God.' The Torah clearly lays down that no one can be condemned on his own admission alone, but Caiaphas was past caring by this stage, and he browbeat the rest of the council members into submission. 'He has blasphemed. What need of witnesses have we now? There! You have just heard the blasphemy. What is your opinion?' In one impatient moment he had sabotaged the carefully laid plans of Annas. He had condemned Jesus to death unlawfully, made a martyr of Him, and caused a backlash whose echoes are still to be heard resonating down the centuries.

***

The disciples of Caiaphas bring the law into disrepute in every generation, and we belong to their number. We demand high Christian standards from others and fail to live up to them ourselves. We take full advantage of the benefits of the law and make little or no contribution to the welfare of the community. We watch in silence while the law is manipulated as long as the manipulation suits us. We demand truthful and upright behaviour from those in the public eye and fail to respect those same standards in our private lives.

Lord, Your hardest words were reserved for those whom You called 'hypocrites' and 'whited sepulchres' – the pretenders to goodness and love. Forgive the insincerity of so many of our words and actions and make us more honest and sincere in our daily service of You.

Pontius Pilate

> They did not go into the Praetorium themselves
> or they would be defiled and unable to eat the
> Passover. So Pilate came outside to them and
> said, 'What charge do you bring against this
> man?'

The scriptures seem to give us a picture of
Pontius Pilate that is strangely at odds with
what we know about him from other sources.
As might be expected, he plays little part in the
life of Jesus up to the time of His trial, and here
he is presented as a peevish but otherwise
well-meaning functionary of the Roman
Empire. Indeed he is seen as a rather sensitive
human being, an honest broker caught up in a
no-win historical situation, who does all he can
to prevent what he knows to be a miscarriage
of justice; and when all his efforts, even his
attempt to buy the Jews off with the scourging
of Jesus, have failed, he solemnly washes his
hands in public and declares that they must
take responsibility for what is about to happen.
Then when Jesus is nailed to the cross he has
an inscription mounted over His head which
he knows will annoy the Jews. And finally,
when approached by Joseph of Arimathea, he
grants permission for the body of Jesus to be
taken down from the cross even though it
would normally have been left hanging there
throughout the Sabbath. All of which leads us
to form a fairly high opinion of Pilate's

intentions, if not of his performance. He is perhaps a weak man, but not malicious.

The Jewish historian Josephus, on the other hand, paints a very different picture. Pilate is not merely ruthless in his account, he is also bigoted and stupid. When he first came to Jerusalem to take up office he deliberately flouted the tradition whereby Roman soldiers did not carry the standards of their legions, which showed carvings of the Emperor, into Jerusalem, in deference to Jewish religious beliefs. In spite of the Jewish outcry, Pilate refused to take them down, but the Jews would not go away and after six days of petition and refusal Pilate finally surrounded them with his soldiers and told them to either desist or die. Instead of running away, the Jews threw themselves on the ground before the soldiers and declared themselves willing to die rather than endure the blasphemy of those pagan idols standing within sight of their temple. Pilate was so impressed that he moved the standards to his palace at Caesarea. On a later occasion, however, when the Jews protested about his use of temple funds to build an aqueduct for the city – and protested this time with a great deal of scurrilous personal abuse – he sent his soldiers disguised among the crowd and killed large numbers of them.

Quite clearly there is no love lost between Pilate and the Jewish leaders. He distrusts their religious zeal and he is tired of their political manoeuvring. To him they are a bunch of fanatics, full of religious prohibitions and practices, always looking for a chance to stir things up against their Roman rulers. Anything that embarrasses them, anything that squeezes them into a corner and forces them to make unpopular decisions is most welcome to Pilate.

If he had wanted he could have spared Christ and scattered the mob without any great effort. In fact, seven years later, he attacked a religious procession of Samaritans at Mount Gerizzim and killed large numbers of them, but in this instance he had to pay the price that he had avoided paying over Christ. He was reported to his superior, Vitellius, and ordered by him to return to Rome and explain his behaviour to the Emperor. It was precisely this kind of fate that Pilate was furiously trying to avoid when he sentenced Jesus to be crucified.

***

Lord, we guard our petty privileges so eagerly. We trifle with the standards and obligations of our own lives, while showing contempt for those who are different from us. We abuse the power we exercise over the lives of others, whether in the workplace or in our own homes. We resist change as though it were an evil when our situation calls out for it. Give us the courage, Lord, to stand upon our Christian values and to apply them fearlessly in every aspect of our lives.

King Herod

> When Pilate heard this, he asked if the man
> were a Galilean; and finding that he came under
> Herod's jurisdiction he passed Him over to
> Herod who was also in Jerusalem at that time.

Herod was a devious and ruthless schemer. No
other title really does him justice. He became
ruler of Galilee by the terms of his father's will,
but he maintained his power by acting as a spy
for the Emperor Tiberius. He kept an eye on the
activities of the Roman officials and the local
kings in the eastern Empire, and if their behaviour did not impress him he sent unfavourable
reports back to the Emperor. This was probably
why Pontius Pilate was his enemy, but even
relatively powerful men like Pilate's boss,
Vitellius, the Legate of Syria, feared him
because he had the ear of the Emperor, and he
did not hesitate to report everything – truth
and fiction – that came his way.

Among the Jewish people he was no more
popular. He had offended their laws and cus-
toms in a particularly off-hand manner by
divorcing his wife to marry Herodias, who was
already married to Philip, another member of
the Herod family. John the Baptist particularly
condemned the marriage and for his pains was
thrown into prison by Herod and later behead-
ed. Indeed, Herod's standing among the Jews
was so poor that even the Pharisees, who were

no friends of Jesus, felt obliged to warn Him that Herod was plotting to kill Him. The news does not seem to have surprised Jesus. He described Herod as 'that fox' and, in so many words, told him not to bother plotting His death because when the time came He would lay down His own life.

This then was the man to whom Pilate sent Jesus in the hope of shifting the responsibility for passing sentence on Him from his own shoulders, especially if a death sentence had to be passed. It would suit his purposes perfectly if a Jew – even a shifty and careless one like Herod – were to pass the sentence of death on Jesus and, thus, allow him to escape the disapproval of the ordinary people who were strongly in favour of Jesus.

Like all dictators, Herod was superstitious. He had killed John the Baptist to fulfil a rash and foolish promise to his step-daughter, and the death lay heavy on his conscience – in so far as anything troubled his conscience – for he knew that John was no ordinary man. Now John's cousin had appeared, doing even more extraordinary things, and Herod was afraid; and he was being called upon to pass a sentence on Him also. It was as if John the Baptist had come back to haunt him.

He questioned Jesus closely about his teaching, and asked for a miracle, but Jesus made no answer whatever. He stood silently before him, and the longer He stood there the more frightened Herod became. There was a power and a majesty about this man that he could not understand. Nonetheless, he could not afford to throw Pilate's gesture of friendship back in his face. He had to find an answer that pleased Pilate and at the same time got rid of Jesus.

He came up with the perfect answer: Make a joke of it! Dress Jesus in fancy robes and send him back to Pilate. Rather like saying, 'These religious fanatics are hilarious. Nobody knows what they'll try next.' And with this gesture of contempt Herod salved his conscience, kept Pilate's friendship, and passed into history as one of the four men responsible for the death of Jesus Christ.

***

Lord, teach us the proper uses of authority. Give us a respect for all people, especially those whom we do not know well. Take away the tendency to despise or laugh at what we do not understand, and the courage to be honest and impartial in all our judgments. Keep us ever mindful that, like you, we 'have come to serve, not to be served', and that by doing so we are fulfilling the highest ideals of your teaching.

Let us pray.

Lord, we have been content to go with the tide of history and lay the death of Jesus at the feet of others, men like Annas, Caiaphas, Pilate and Herod, but we have all had a share in His death for we have all been guilty of the evils for which He died. Help us to realise that He died for each one of us, and the enmity between one man and another – for whatever reason – is a betrayal of the sacrifice of Christ on the cross and of our dignity as God's children. If we cannot love our enemies as we should, at least teach us to pray for them so that God will bless them in every way. May their hearts be uplifted and their minds enlightened so that they can forgive us our sins against them, and together may we find peace in this life and eternal joy in the next. This we ask through Christ our Lord.

Amen.

Good Friday III

The Victim

On a barren hillside, known locally as the Skull, some 2000 years ago, an ordinary man named Joshua, or Jesus, son of Joseph and Mary, was put to death for disturbing the peace and threatening the operation of stable and peaceful government.

On that same hillside, Jesus, the Son of God, Creator of the Universe, King of Kings and Lord of Lords, became a frail man among other men, offered His life as a sacrifice of atonement, as a means of reconciliation with God for the sins of all mankind.

To unbelievers, He was a man of immense charm and spiritual insight, a man of vision, a man of courage and sensitivity, but, for all that, He was a man, and was put to death on Good Friday.

To believers, the Son of God himself, having entered the human race through conception and birth, took upon himself responsibility for our sins and offered to God the Father his own life on the cross.

No human logic or reasoning can make us believe this. Like the Son of God himself, our faith is a gift from God the Father, a gift that we can treasure and protect, or a gift that we can squander and eventually lose, but for those with faith Good Friday has only one meaning – the death of Jesus the Son of God for our sakes.

The Arrest

Jesus has taken a few chosen friends with him to a quiet garden, where he can face the terror of his impending death. He wants to be alone, as we all want to be alone with our fears. 'My soul is sorrowful to the point of death,' he tells them. 'Wait here and keep awake with me.' Then, moving away from them, he kneels and bows his face to the ground in the traditional eastern posture of prayer. The fear of death is like no other fear, but the fear of pain and torture that will lead to his death intensifies it beyond endurance. 'Father, if it is possible, let this cup pass me by. Nevertheless, let it be as You, not I, would have it.' He has come to do His father's will, and nothing, not even the fear of pain and death, must prevent Him.

Slowly he steels himself for the fate that lies ahead. He returns to His disciples, pale and tight-lipped, like a man walking to the gallows. 'Sleep on now and take your rest. My betrayer is already close at hand.'

Judas, his trusted friend and follower for the past three years, has guided the temple guards and the Roman soldiers to where he can be found, and now they surround him with swords and clubs at the ready, prepared, as they had been told, to capture a violent revolutionary whose ambition was to destroy the temple and their God-given way of life. Even when he speaks calmly to them, admitting his identity and asking only that his followers be allowed to go free, they step back carefully keeping a discreet distance between themselves and this dangerous criminal. He has escaped before, and this time there must be no mistake, so they close in on him cautiously and tie his hands behind his back before leading him away.

***

Where does our hatred, our fear of one another spring from? Why has the image of the pale prisoner with strained face and hands tied behind him, being led off into captivity, become so familiar? We have done it so often, and we still do it so often, that each age has enlisted the skill of its craftsmen to produce a bond that is more reliable, a manacle that is more enduring, a handcuff that is more adaptable, until we come to the ultimate irony of our own age – no longer a manacle that is crafted for the individual, nor even a handcuff that can bind you today and me tomorrow, but a disposable bond that has grown out of man's ingenious manipulation and control of the fuels of the earth. A man-made fibre, but not made to clothe our bodies or to protect our food, but woven into strips that will bind the hands of the eternal prisoner behind him, marketed like any other product for its convenience and durability. We have unlocked the mysteries of the atom merely to produce a more effective bond with which to tie our neighbour's hands behind him.

Lord, bring an end to the wars of the world, so that we will no longer see the frightened faces of captives being led off into the unknown; disposable men in their disposable bonds.

The Blow

Jesus is led from the Garden of Gethsemane by the temple guards and Roman soldiers, not to the house of Caiaphas the High Priest, nor to the Palace of Pilate the Roman Governor, but the house of Annas, the father-in-law of Caiaphas and the real power behind the throne. His son-in-law Caiaphas was only one of the many whom he had manoeuvred into the position of High Priest, among them his five sons and his grandson. It was to Annas that Jesus was brought in the darkness of night and questioned about his teaching and about the men who followed him.

His answer to the questions was direct, almost to the point of belligerence. 'I have spoken openly for all the world to hear; I have always taught in the synagogue and in the temple where all the Jews meet together. I have said nothing in secret. But why ask me? Ask my hearers what I taught; they know what I said.'

It was not the answer his audience had expected. They were used to prisoners picking their words carefully and avoiding offence, especially when they were hauled before the authorities in the middle of the night, but this prisoner was neither fawning nor afraid. He defied them, and even shook them with his calm dignity, for it seemed to highlight the fact that they had already broken the law by using an informer and by arresting him during the night. The former High Priest would not soil his hands by striking a prisoner, but his servants knew his mind only too well, and one of them struck Jesus a blow across the face and reminded him just who he was talking to. 'Is that the way to answer the High Priest?'

Once again, the response defeated them. It was neither angry nor frightened. It was calm and reasonable. 'If there is something wrong in what I said, point it out; but if there is no offence in it, why do you strike me?'

Annas had no answer. His bullying tactics had failed. He could only send Jesus on to Caiaphas and hope that the guardians of the law would be more successful than the guardians of power in trapping this upstart.

***

How rarely do we live out our lives without suffering an unjust blow. If we suffer it as children we probably have to endure in silence, but it is folded away in the recesses of our minds along with the embarrassment and the resentment; and if we suffer it as adults then we probably strike back; or if the enemy is too powerful we plan revenge for another time. We nurse the resentment until it festers in our hearts and spreads like an infection into every corner of our lives. And from us the infection spreads to another generation, for children learn by our words and our example and our silence that they can get what they want much quicker by bullying and threatening than by working or waiting. Violence has become the accepted substitute for understanding, compassion, patience and guidance. A slap, a blow, a beating up, a maiming, or a crippling are the quick response, but not the answer, to all the complicated problems of life: I do not need to be right or wise or just; I only need to be bigger and stronger and more ruthless than you, and I can make you submit to my will.

Lord, when you accepted pain and suffering at the hands of violent men you became one with all the battered children, beaten wives, broken prisoners, and all the other countless victims of violence. Heal their wounds Lord, and teach us compassion.

The Crowning with Thorns

Jesus is taken before Pilate, the Roman Governor, the ultimate authority. With him rests the power to condemn Jesus or to set Him free. But power is dearly bought, and cannot be gambled on mere questions of right and wrong.

Pilate has already used up his meagre store of goodwill in Rome. He has acted rashly on several occasions already, letting his violent temper run loose and using the sword when he should have used his head. To the mob, which now confronts him, he is the Roman Governor, but to men like Annas and Herod and Caiaphas, he is merely another paid official whose career can be undermined by a few discreet words in the right ear in Rome.

For a time Pilate stalls. Never has he been confronted with such an unlikely criminal – a man who dismisses the ambitions of the world so lightly, and proclaims himself king of an eternal land. He tries to do a deal, to make them an offer they cannot refuse – a full pardon for one of their own on the eve of the Passover – but the offer merely betrays his weakness. They throw it back in his face and demand instead the release of Barabbas, a criminal by any standards.

Pilate has only one more card to play. He will punish Jesus so severely that common humanity will demand his release, even if justice will not. He hands Him over to his soldiers, who scourge His back with whips and in a final act of brutal mockery, place a crown of thorns on His head.

***

Every generation has found its own way to repress the workings of the human mind. Every age has woven its own crown of thorns to place upon the heads of those who disagree, who question, who search, who think, and the prophecy becomes self-fulfilling: 'With desolation is the land made desolate, because there is no one that thinketh in his heart.'

The prophet, the visionary, the innovator frightens us. He brings changes and we are not prepared – not at the moment, anyway – to give up our smoothly running and comfortable way of life or of government or of prayer or whatever for a system that is untried, unknown and unlikely, in our estimation, to work. So we mock the innovator.

We laugh at what we do not understand, and we brand new ideas as dangerous. And if the thinkers and the prophets and the visionaries cannot be silenced by mockery then we resort to more underhand techniques. We suggest that these strange people who keep putting forward unconventional views are really ambitious people trying to undermine our traditional values and subvert the workings of good government. They are dangerous and ought to be watched carefully, or restricted in their activities, or locked away for their own good. We must not have new ideas rolling around like loose cannons on the deck of life. When a head is raised above the parapet we place a crown of thorns on it.

Lord, let me see a little further into the mysteries of life, and give me courage to support the visionaries and the enthusiasts who alone can lead our minds from ignorance into enlightenment, and who so often must go through life with a crown of thorns upon their heads.

The Crucifixion

Pilate is convinced that the Jewish demand for the death of Jesus is more of a personal vendetta than a desire for justice. He thinks that by humiliating and punishing Jesus he will present them with such a pathetic figure that they will instinctively agree to His release. If nothing else, His physical wounds will take so long to heal the He will make no trouble for them for a long time to come.

His irritation and his disappointment are all the more pronounced when he finds that he has made no impression on them whatsoever. 'Here is the man,' he calls to them. Here is the stark fulfilment of Isaiah's prophecy. 'Without beauty, without majesty (we saw him), no looks to attract our eyes; a thing despised and rejected by men, a man of sorrows and familiar with suffering, a man to make people screen their faces.'

Pilate turns back to Jesus, puzzled, and just a little afraid. Who is this man who has aroused such passions? 'Where do you come from?' he asks. But Jesus has finished with the pointless answers. They might disturb Pilate's conscience, but they will not change his mind.

It takes the ultimate threat to make Pilate give way: 'If you set Him free you are no friend of Caesar.' He could not afford to offend Caesar, but he could make the chief priests and the other Jewish leaders pay for their victory. 'Will I crucify your King?' he asks. And they reply with the ultimate lie – for a Jew, the final falsehood: 'We have no king but Caesar.' So in the end, we are told, Pilate handed Jesus over to them to be crucified.

***

The efforts of Pilate to set Jesus free are completely at odds with the character of the man as we know it from history. But the behaviour of tyrants has always been unpredictable; at one moment consigning thousands to their deaths without a shiver, at another weeping inconsolably over the death of a pet dog. Only their love of power is common to them all. To retain it, they have spared no one, neither enemies nor friends, not even their own families.

And we, in spite of all our protestations, have walked meekly in their footsteps. We have sacrificed truth and principle and ultimately life itself in the pursuit of power. We may call it by another name, and we may wash our hands like Pilate and proclaim that we are innocent of the blood of this man, but we have spoken when we should have kept silent and kept silent when we should have spoken, and given credibility and even respect to those who claim to act in our name. We have not spoken fearlessly for the truth, the truth that is Christ's teaching, the truth that will set us free.

Lord, give us courage to stand up before your enemies, to speak your truth fearlessly before all, to admit our waywardness in the past, and to live out your commandment to love our neighbour as ourselves.

Let us pray.

Reach out this day, O Lord, to all who are suffering, especially to those like yourself who are suffering at the hands of their fellow men. Enlighten the minds of all mankind so that they may strive to be like you 'gentle and humble of heart'. Give new courage to those who are weighed down by their sufferings, console those who are lonely and depressed, give new health to those who are sick, stand close to those who are bereaved or deserted, and bring us all in due time to that eternal happiness where we will live by the spirit and praise you and the Father forever and ever.

Amen.

A Meditation on the Seven Last Words of Jesus from the Cross

Jesus, Lord and Saviour, you gave yourself up to a cruel death on the cross for our sakes, and from the cross you still speak to us words of guidance and comfort. Our own shallow experience tells us how important any man's last words are, how free from the selfishness that taints our lives, and from the cautious care that we take before revealing ourselves they are. Only in the face of death can we confront the harsh truth of our lives, and express the convictions of our hearts without fear of rejection or hope of gain.

How much more powerful, Lord, must your words be, spoken from the cross as you faced death? Help us to appreciate these vital words, and to make of them not just a touching memorial of your passion, but a source of inspiration and guidance and truth.

The First Word

FATHER FORGIVE THEM: THEY DO NOT KNOW WHAT THEY ARE DOING

During His public life Jesus has dumbfounded his listeners, especially the Jewish authorities, by preaching a doctrine of love and forgiveness. No longer would it be enough to love your friends and hate your enemies, nor to seek an eye for an eye and a tooth for a tooth, nor to forgive a man just once or twice, or even seven times, but seventy times seven times. He has pardoned the woman taken in adultery. He has defended the disciples who plucked the ears of corn on the Sabbath day. He has sat down at the table with publicans and sinners, and even forgiven His chosen successor who denied that he ever knew Him. His teaching is a stumbling block to the Jews and madness to the pagans, and even now as He hangs upon the cross He must continue to proclaim that theme which has lain at the heart of all His teaching: forgiveness.

***

Lord Jesus, teach me to love even those who have offended me. Guide my mind and my heart so that I may look beneath the appearances and learn to appreciate every person for what he/she is, not just a weak and sinful human being, but a child of God, loved by the father, and worthy of redemption by Your death on the cross. Help me to look beyond the hurts that I have suffered and the grievances that I have nursed, so that I may judge no one lest I be judged myself, and nourish in me a spirit of forgiveness so that I may pardon others as I hope one day to be pardoned.

The Second Word

TODAY YOU WILL BE WITH ME IN PARADISE

As Jesus hangs upon the cross there is little sympathy from the crowd that surrounds Him. The Roman soldiers sit below Him, drinking their wine and dividing His clothes among them. Further back, the merchants and money-changers are enjoying their revenge, and back in the city the Jewish leaders are triumphant, for they need no longer fear His power or His words.

Beside Him, one of the thieves joins in the general condemnation. He can only think of his own terrible predicament, and he demands to know why Jesus cannot save Himself and them as well. But his companion has sensed some of the dignity of Jesus. He knows that this man is no common criminal. He knows that charges of blasphemy are rarely pursued to their extremes by the authorities unless there is a hidden reason. He turns and offers to Jesus the most poignant and powerful prayer ever uttered: 'Lord, remember me when You come into Your kingdom.' In return he is rewarded with immediate salvation: 'Today you will be with me in paradise.'

***

Remember all of us, Lord, here below as we stumble along life's journey, weighed down by the burden of our sins and the confusion of our own wayward desires. It is a journey of disappointment and disillusionment; disappointment with ourselves and disillusionment with the world we have created, for the visions which inspired our youth and the goals which we so confidently set, have remained unfulfilled. Increase our faith, Lord, so that no matter how far we have strayed from You, and no matter how hopeless the task that confronts us, we will turn to You with undimmed confidence and make our own the prayer of the thief on the cross: 'Lord remember me when You come into Your kingdom.'

The Third Word

WOMAN, BEHOLD THY SON
SON, BEHOLD THY MOTHER

The angry mob have followed Jesus to the hill of Calvary, jeering and shouting at Him as he stumbles along. For a while they stand on the summit in a frenzy of meaningless hatred. But their anger is soon dissipated. There is no satisfaction in abusing someone who does not respond. There is only a growing sense of guilt. One by one they drift away, back to the city and their homes and the preparations of the coming Sabbath Day. Only then does a small group of believers approach the cross to see what has been done to their leader. The mother of Jesus, her sister Mary of Cleophas, Mary Magdalene and His beloved disciple, John, all look with silent horror at the blood-stained figure of Jesus. No words can express their pain and their desolation. John supports the mother of Jesus as she moves closer to her son, and from the cross He speaks to both of them: 'Woman behold thy son. Son behold thy mother.'

***

Lord Jesus, it is hard for us to believe that You have won sure and certain salvation for us; that by Your birth from Mary You have taken upon Yourself our human nature with all its fragility and openness to sin; that by Your passion You have taken upon Yourself all the sins and sufferings of the world; and that by Your death and resurrection You have offered to the Father the one true sacrifice which takes away the sins of the world.

Lord, we are tempted to justify ourselves by parading our virtues. Increase, instead, our humility, so that we can pray with all God's children: 'Lord, be merciful to me a sinner.'

The Fourth Word

MY GOD, MY GOD, WHY HAVE YOU FORSAKEN ME?

As he hangs upon the cross Jesus turns to the prayer of His youth, and offers to His Father the words of a psalm; familiar words, but prophetic also, for they foretell the events that will lead to the fate of the Messiah. The earth has trembled, the sun has been darkened and the crowds who have been jeering and reviling Him are now scurrying home 'beating their breasts'. He has been vindicated by the very clouds in the sky, but the people to whom He has come, the honoured guests whom He has invited into His Father's house, have all turned away. Peter has denied Him, Judas has betrayed Him, the other Apostles have deserted Him. The Jews have jeered at Him, the Romans have scourged Him, Herod has laughed at Him and Pilate has abandoned Him. He has been beaten and crowned with thorns and kept without sleep, loaded with a cross and dragged up the hill to Calvary, and crucified. The prayer of Jesus from the cross is no longer a thing of mere words but a cry from the heart, for it seems to him that now even the Father has abandoned Him.

***

Lord, how terrifying life can be. How desolate we feel when the friends and familiar faces are taken away from us in death, and how much more desolate when they seem to desert us in times of crisis. There is no one to whom we can turn; no one to whom we can open our hearts and reveal the secret fears that torment us; no one to wait patiently with us; no one to put a supporting arm around us until we have found the courage to face an empty world again.

Have pity, Lord, on all the lonely people: the sick in the loneliness of their hospital bed; the poor in the loneliness of their empty room; the exiles in the loneliness of a strange land; the workers in the loneliness of a crowded city; the young in the loneliness of their frightened selves; and the old in the loneliness of approaching death. Have pity on them all, and hear their prayer, Lord, as they cry out to all of us: 'Why have you forsaken me?'

The Fifth Word

I THIRST

As He journeyed up and down the Jordan Valley under a scorching sun, Jesus must have known something of the agony of real thirst – the burning sweat, the cracked lips and the dizzy faintness that finally overtakes the body. At any rate, He used the image to great effect in His teaching, and assured His followers that if they gave a cup of cold water to the needy they would not lose their reward.

As He hangs now upon the cross, one of the Roman soldiers reaps that reward as he responds to the cry of Jesus. He soaks a sponge in the coarse wine which they have been drinking at the foot of the cross, and holds it to the mouth of Jesus. In fulfilment of the prophetic words of the psalm, He tastes the wine, and having done so He turns away from the world and resigns Himself to the will of his Father.

***

Jesus, we have watched you expend Yourself without stint for the salvation of the human race. When You changed water into wine for the thirsty wedding guests, and multiplied the loaves and fishes for the hungry crowds, You did not even have a place where You could lay Your head to rest. When You gave way to the relentless demands of the crowds because they were like sheep without a shepherd, You were so exhausted that You slept soundly through a storm that made Your disciples fear for their lives. On the only occasion when You asked for a drink of water for Yourself, it was merely the pretext for bringing a woman who had strayed back to the awareness that God still loves even those whom the world has rejected.

Lord, let Your spirit take a more active control of my life, so that like You, I will thirst for the well-being of others and become more forgetful of myself.

The Sixth Word

IT IS ACCOMPLISHED

From the start of His public life Jesus' only goal has been to do the will of the Father. 'I have come from heaven, not to do my own will but the will of Him who sent me.' In the eyes of the world, He has been a failure. His home town, Nazareth, has been scandalised by His behaviour. The people of Capernaum will walk with Him no more. Galilee has become unsafe for Him. Jerusalem has plotted to put Him to death. Yet, He can still tell His Apostles as He meets with them for the last time, 'I have finished the work that the Father gave me to do.'

***

Lord, how hard it is to find people who will listen to Your word. We are so caught up in the petty details of life – the struggle for success, the search for wealth and power and the so-called necessities of life. As You looked down on the City of Jerusalem You wept bitter tears because You would have sheltered those people as a hen shelters her chicks under her wings, but no one paid any attention. They were too busy with important matters. One had bought a farm, another was trying out a new pair of oxen, a third had married a wife.

Lord, help us to listen and be guided by You so that no matter where or in what situation we find ourselves, we will be able to repeat with You: 'I have finished the work that you gave me to do. It is accomplished.'

The Seventh Word

INTO YOUR HANDS, O LORD, I COMMIT MY SPIRIT

The work that the Father has given Him to do is now completed. Jesus knows that it has all the appearances of failure. His Apostles have deserted Him because they thought He had lost. Judas has betrayed Him because the only Messiah he can believe in is a conqueror. If Jesus had overcome His enemies once again and marched in triumph into Jerusalem, Judas would have followed Him.

Instead, Jesus has been crucified, and as He hangs upon the cross, alone and desolate, He returns to the prayers and the sacred writings of His youth once again: 'In You, Lord, I put my trust; I say, "You are my God." My fortunes are in Your hands; rescue me from the power of my enemies and those who persecute me.'

***

Lord, we live in a world that has no time for failure. We trample down the gentle and humble of heart, and believe that the powerful will possess the land. We have turned away from the cross and put our faith in power and human persuasion.

Open our hearts to the truth, Lord, so that we can believe in a beaten Messiah, and make

our own the words of the prophet Isaiah:
'Ours were the sufferings He bore, ours the
sorrows He carried. But we, we thought of
Him as someone punished, struck by God,
and brought low. Yet, He was pierced through
for our faults, crushed for our sins. On Him
lies a punishment that brings us peace, and
through His wounds we are healed.'

Let us pray.

Lord Jesus, You accepted death at the hands of sinful men so that by Your resurrection from the dead You might free all of us from our sins. Keep us mindful of the high price that You paid for our redemption, and of the glorious victory which You won over sin and death. Without Your death and resurrection we would still be lost in our sins, desperately seeking forgiveness, and vainly searching for meaning to this life, and for hope of eternal life. May we always be faithful to the ideals of charity, forgiveness, and humility which You taught, and ever opposed to the selfish and short-sighted values that surround us. May we find the courage to be truly Christian in our outlook, and to commit ourselves wholeheartedly to You, 'the way, the truth and the life'.

Stations of the Cross

Dear Jesus,

We come together today to walk with You in spirit along the Way of the Cross. Our sins and the sins of mankind have brought You to this torment. We have gone astray, like sheep, unthinking and selfish, following the ways of our sinful natures, and the empty deceits of this sinful world. This walk of death is the price You paid to save us from a just punishment.

Open our minds and hearts this day, O Lord, so that we may catch a glimpse of the agony You endured for us, and having once perceived it may we never cease to thank You for Your infinite mercy and compassion.

The First Station

JESUS IS CONDEMNED TO DEATH

We adore You, O Christ, and we praise You because by Your holy cross You have redeemed the world.

Jesus stands before Pilate, a beaten, blood-stained figure. Around Him, a raging mob is shouting, 'Kill Him, Crucify Him.' Pilate despises the mob, but he cannot risk the Emperor's anger. He cannot release a man who claims to be the King of the Jews. So he gives way to cowardice and ambition, and hands Jesus over to them to be crucified.

***

Jesus, my Lord, I have taken the easy choice so often, and betrayed my deepest beliefs for a moment of pleasure, or a moment of glory. I have deserted You in Your hour of need, and found a 'Pilate' to take the blame. Lord, make me see my own weakness, and help me to stand up for You, no matter who else may fail You.

The Second Station

JESUS CARRIES HIS CROSS

We adore You, O Christ, and we praise You because by Your holy cross You have redeemed the world.

A squad of Roman soldiers drags Jesus onto the road leading out of the city, and sets the heavy beam of the cross upon his shoulders. It is a rough, carelessly hacked length of timber, that carries in its grain the life-blood of previous victims who died on it. Behind Him come the two thieves also carrying their cross-beams, pathetic ambassadors of the human race walking towards death, barely aware that Jesus is leading them.

***

Lord, how bitterly we complain about our own crosses in life, and how easily we forget that it was our sins that set the heavy weight of the cross on Your shoulders. But You wanted to convince us of the depth of Your love for us, and so You led the way, through suffering and death, into the glory of eternal life.

The Third Station

JESUS FALLS THE FIRST TIME

We adore You, O Christ, and we praise You because by Your holy cross You have redeemed the world.

Jesus has been scourged with a whip of leather thongs, His head has been crowned with thorns, and He has been casually beaten and abused by the soldiers. His friends have all deserted Him. Little wonder then that the cross weighs heavily on His shoulder; little wonder then that He stumbles and falls to the ground.

***

Lord, how hard we find it to forgive ourselves for our failures. We would prefer to be saints who never fall and who do not need forgiveness. Help us to realise that You still love us, and that You came to save us even while we were still sinners.

The Fourth Station

JESUS MEETS HIS BLESSED MOTHER

We adore You, O Christ, and we praise You because by Your holy cross You have redeemed the world.

The crowd watches impassively as Jesus passes by. Another Messiah has come and gone. Some of His disciples follow behind, hoping that, even yet, He will overcome His executioners. His mother, Mary, stands silently by the wayside, heedless of victory or defeat, merely aware that her beloved son is stumbling past her on His way to execution.

***

Lord, it is so hard to watch the sufferings of someone we love, yet Mary could only stand by the way and watch the sufferings of her son. If you allow Your mother to carry such a weight of suffering, why should You expect any less from me?

The Fifth Station

SIMON HELPS JESUS TO CARRY THE CROSS

We adore You, O Christ, and we praise You because by Your holy cross You have redeemed the world.

No one steps from the crowd to help the stumbling Jesus. These are honest, God-fearing people. The festival of Passover is approaching, and they must not defile themselves with the touch of a criminal. The soldiers care nothing for them or for Jesus, for He is a condemned criminal, and it is their job to see that He dies on the cross, not along the wayside. They pull Simon of Cyrene from the crowd and order him to carry the cross ahead of Jesus.

***

Lord, You know how rarely we choose to pick up the cross. The world tells us that we should be free to enjoy ourselves, so we avoid the cross till You set it on our shoulders and say, 'If you would come after me, you must take up your cross daily and follow me.' Only then do we learn that the cross of service and suffering is a vital part of our daily lives.

The Sixth Station

VERONICA WIPES THE FACE OF JESUS

We adore You, O Christ, and we praise You because by Your holy cross You have redeemed the world.

An ancient tradition tells us that a woman stepped from the crowd and wiped the sweat and blood from the face of Jesus with a towel. Perhaps she was one of that wealthy group of women who made the care of condemned criminals their apostolate. At any rate, she was a woman of great compassion and courage. She did not see a hardened criminal before her; she saw a son, or a father, or a brother, in less fortunate circumstances, and so she stepped boldly forward to help.

***

Lord, how hard it is for us to step out from the crowd. We dream of blazing new trails, but we worry about being hated or even laughed at. Lord, give us courage to speak out for what we believe in, to risk the mockery and even the contempt of the crowd, and step forward like Veronica to console the suffering Jesus, wherever He may be found today.

The Seventh Station

JESUS FALLS THE SECOND TIME

We adore You, O Christ, and we praise You because by Your holy cross You have redeemed the world.

As He climbs the narrowing street to Calvary, Jesus is continually pushed and jostled by the crowd. He can scarcely see where He is going and loss of blood has left Him dizzy and confused. He tries to blot out the uproar and the insults of the crowd, but neither mind nor body can respond to His wishes, and He falls to the ground a second time.

***

Lord, You have watched us fall and rise again, from childhood to the present day. We do not want to sin, but the selfish impulses and the evil longings are as strong as ever. Perhaps the opportunities are fewer, but we still fall frequently, and we still depend on You to raise us up, and to help us struggle on again as You did on the road to Calvary.

The Eight Station

JESUS SPEAKS TO THE WOMEN OF JERUSALEM

We adore You, O Christ, and we praise You because by Your holy cross You have redeemed the world.

The crowds surround Jesus on all sides. Most are hurling abuse and insults at Him, but here and there little groups weep for Him, for He is a sad and pitiful sight. Their concern touches Him, and, in spite of His agony, Jesus speaks to them and warns them of the destruction to come. 'Women of Jerusalem do not weep for me; weep rather for yourselves and for your children.'

***

Lord, we have never been good at forgetting our own pain. We have not the courage or the control to set aside our own suffering for a moment, and pay attention to the needs of others. On the road to death, You forgot Your own sufferings, and stopped to speak to the women who wept for You. Make me more generous, Lord. Make me more willing to use the gifts that You have given me, so that they may benefit others rather than just protect myself.

The Ninth Station

JESUS FALLS THE THIRD TIME

We adore You, O Christ, and we praise You because by Your holy cross You have redeemed the world.

As He approaches the summit of Calvary Jesus is barely conscious of what is happening. He can no longer focus on the ground before Him. The soldiers push and prod Him onwards, and the crowd surges forward so as to be in place for the kill. Try as He may, He can no longer demand the obedience of His weary limbs. The last few steps are too steep, and He falls a third time to the ground.

***

Lord, we expect You to be reasonable. As we grow older we expect You to lighten the burdens and to lift the temptations, but You allow us to be tried and tempted right to the bitter end. Strengthen us, Lord, on this last stretch of the journey, so that we may persevere to the end, and eventually find peace with You.

The Tenth Station

JESUS IS STRIPPED OF HIS GARMENTS

We adore You, O Christ, and we praise You because by Your holy cross You have redeemed the world.

The squad of Roman soldiers rips the garments from Jesus, for He is a criminal and He must die naked. That is the law. Crucifixion is a coarse and brutal business, with no place for sympathy or compassion. The soldiers quickly divide up the garments among them, and then get on with the execution.

***

Lord, how carefully we maintain a bold front, and present an appearance of generous piety to the world, and yet we know that the day is coming when You will look into our hearts and see there the sinfulness that we have so carefully concealed. Help us, Lord, to see ourselves today as we really are, so that we may confront our sinfulness, and change to what is pleasing to You.

The Eleventh Station

JESUS IS NAILED TO THE CROSS

We adore You, O Christ, and we praise You because by Your holy cross You have redeemed the world.

The cross-beam is laid on the ground and Jesus is stretched out upon it. A soldier holds each hand in turn while his comrade hammers a heavy nail through the flesh and into the wood. Then He is lifted onto the upright, which already stands in place, and the nails are driven into His feet. Then more nails and rope secure the cross beam and upright together. Finally, a rope is tied around His chest so that He cannot struggle and perhaps break free, and, thus, He is left to die.

***

Lord, we do not want to be nailed to the cross, nor do we want the cross to be nailed to us. We do not want to carry the burdens that You have laid upon us – crosses of sickness, financial crosses, domestic crosses, crosses of bereavement, crosses of betrayal, crosses of depression and despair. So often, Lord, my cross will seem the heaviest. When that happens, remind me that Your cross was freely taken up, and that in it You bore the weight of all mankind's sinfulness, but especially of mine.

The Twelfth Station

JESUS DIED ON THE CROSS

We adore You, O Christ, and we praise You because by Your holy cross You have redeemed the world.

Crucifixion is a slow and painful death, and while Jesus hung upon the cross the chief priests and the scribes stood before Him and jeered, 'He saved others, He cannot save Himself.' For a moment, the utter hopelessness of His task overpowers Him, and He cries out in agony, 'My God, my God, why have you deserted me.' Then, from a totally unexpected quarter, comes a ray of hope. One of the thieves turns to Him and says, 'Lord remember me when You come into Your kingdom.' All is not lost; there are still those who believe. And having assured him that he would be with Him this day in paradise, Jesus turns to the Father in peace: 'Into your hands, O Lord, I commit my spirit.'

***

Lord, it is hard for us to realise that You gave up Your life for our sakes, that the Son of God came down on this earth and endured bitter sufferings and death to save us from our sins. There were other sinners, we know, Lord, but You would have done it for us if we had been the only sinners, for the will of the Father who sent You was that You should lose nothing of all that He has given to You, but that You should raise it up on the last day.

The Thirteenth Station

JESUS IS TAKEN DOWN FROM THE CROSS

We adore You, O Christ, and we praise You because by Your holy cross You have redeemed the world.

The weakened body of Jesus survived only three hours on the cross, and those who had deserted Him tried to redeem themselves in some small way by sparing no effort or expense in their care for the body of Jesus. Apart from John, only the women had stood fast at the foot of the cross, but now, as they released the body of Jesus from the cross, they all rushed to play their part, and tenderly passed it down into the arms of Mary, His mother, and the other women who stood waiting silently below.

***

How tenderly everyone handled You, Lord, as they brought You down from the cross. We are so much more respectful of the dead than of the living. We tell ourselves, 'If I had been there, Lord, I would have treated You kindly.' But You are here with us, Lord, even in the least of Your brethren, and yet how carelessly we still treat You. Only Your mother showed the same loving care of You in life and in death. Teach us to imitate her, and to respect all Your children at all times.

The Fourteenth Station

THE BODY OF JESUS IS LAID IN THE TOMB

We adore You, O Christ, and we praise You because by Your holy cross You have redeemed the world.

The disciples who had fled at the arrest of Jesus all returned to bury Him. Even those who hesitated to be seen with Him in life felt safe to honour Him in death. Joseph of Arimathea, Nicodemus, even Peter and the other disciples, all took their places behind the body of Jesus and followed it to the tomb. Nonetheless, the funeral was a hurried affair, because they were all God-fearing men, and the Passover preparation day was nearly ended, and the Sabbath must not be broken; so they hurried the body of Jesus to the newly carved tomb, anointed the body, rolled a stone over the entrance and came away.

***

How hard we find it, Lord, to think of the tomb as a beginning and not an end. We are so engrossed with the things of the world that we cannot look beyond this short and sinful life to the wonder of eternity. As You taught us to rise above our worldly nature in life, so now teach us to be ready to follow You through death, so that when at last You call us to Yourself, You may find us ready and waiting, prepared to leave behind this temporary dwelling, and to come to You, and live with You, for all eternity.

Dear Jesus,

We have followed You along the path to Calvary, but not too closely lest we be seen as Your followers and liable to arrest. We have left the courageous gestures to the women – to Veronica who stepped fearlessly forward to mop the brow of Jesus, to the women of Jerusalem who did not hesitate to express their disapproval, to Mary who stood by the cross as her son was dying. We, on the other hand, have kept a safe distance because we fear for our lives and we have little faith. Deepen our shallow faith and teach us to put our trust in You at all times, no matter what we encounter.